The Idiot

FREDERICK BATEMAN

1897

TABLE OF CONTENTS

PREFACE TO THE SECOND EDITION

As stated in the preface to the first edition, the arguments contained in this essay formed the nucleus of an address advocating the claims of the Idiot upon the philanthropists of East Anglia, at a public meeting held in Norwich, in support of the Eastern Counties' Asylum for Idiots, under the presidency of His Grace the Duke of Norfolk, K.G., Earl Marshal of England.

In acceding to the request of the Board of Directors to publish a second edition, I have thought it right to retain the form of a public oration, as requiring less modification in the phraseology of the appeal for help, than would otherwise have been necessary.

Much additional matter has been added, especially in reference to Consanguine Marriages, Parental Intemperance, Overpressure in Education, and other factors in the causation of Idiocy.

I have tried to show how the study of the Idiot is calculated to throw light upon the abstruse question of the connection between Matter and Mind, and that it is a subject fraught with interest not only to the Philanthropist, but to the Theologian, and to the Political Economist.

Although I have endeavoured to explain my views in popular language, I trust it has not been at the sacrifice of strict scientific accuracy.

FREDERIC BATEMAN.
Norwich,
January, 1897.

FREDERICK BATEMAN

THE IDIOT

HIS PLACE IN CREATION, AND HIS CLAIMS ON SOCIETY.

As Consulting Physician to the Eastern Counties' Asylum for Idiots, it is my privilege to advocate the claims of one of the most important charities connected with the Eastern District of England, and which, as such, is calculated to excite an especial interest amongst the philanthropists of East Anglia.

The Eastern Counties' Asylum for Idiots is an institution founded specially for the reception of patients from Norfolk and the three other Eastern Counties, just in the same way as the Royal Albert Asylum, at Lancaster, is intended for patients from the seven northern counties. It is, therefore, essentially an East Anglian Charity, and I dwell especially on this point, because, being situated at Colchester, I think there is an impression in certain quarters, that this institution is less intimately connected with this locality than some other charities, the claims of which are periodically brought under our notice. I feel that the managing body themselves have been to blame for this impression, from having in the first instance adopted the ill-advised name of Essex Hall—a name, however, now abandoned, as tending to convey the impression that it was an Essex charity, whereas, as I have before said, it is an institution intended for the care and treatment of Idiots from the four Eastern Counties of Norfolk, Suffolk, Cambridge, and Essex.

I have so often been called upon to plead the cause of this charity before a Norfolk audience, that I should have preferred that some other person had been selected to represent the Asylum at this meeting; for when the subject of the appeal is always the same, it is difficult to prevent one's thoughts from occasionally running in a similar channel as on former occasions; the Board of Directors having, however, invited me to act as one of their deputation, I acceded to their request with the greater readiness, as it affords me the opportunity, on the part of the authorities of the Asylum, of expressing our grateful thanks to his Grace the Duke of Norfolk for the honour he has done us by his presence here to-day, thus evincing the interest he takes in the charitable institutions of the county, by consenting to preside over a public meeting in the historical city of Norwich.

In the few words that I shall address to you, I wish particularly to avoid falling into the error common to many speakers—that of exaggerating the importance of the subject they are treating. Many a good cause has been damaged by the indiscretion of its own advocates, who, in their undue zeal, endeavour to impress their audiences with the notion that the particular charity for which they plead is the one above all others that has a paramount claim on the support of a philanthropic public. Now, I have no desire to produce a sensational effect, or to create an artificial interest in my subject by indulging in the language of hyperbole. I have a plain unvarnished tale to tell, that requires no meretricious adornment to arrest your attention, for I am here to plead the cause of an unfortunate branch of the human family, who, by the very nature of their infirmity, are unable to say a single word for themselves, and whose mute appeal must excite universal sympathy.

Happily, we live in an age when the spirit of philanthropy is abroad, and all that Christian sympathy can suggest is being done to relieve the sick and suffering poor. Amidst all the boasted culture of antiquity there existed no hospital; go to Athens and to Rome, those seats of early civilization, and you will find at the former the ruins of the Acropolis, and those of the Coliseum at the latter, but no trace of the remains of a hospital or asylum; whereas in the present day, hospitals and asylums are springing up in every locality, and East Anglia is certainly no exception to the rule, abounding, as it does, in charitable institutions of every description, the object of which is to improve the condition of the labouring class, and to lessen the ills that flesh is heir to; and it may truly be said, as far as this country is concerned, that—

"The quality of mercy is not strain'd;
It droppeth, as the gentle rain from heaven
Upon the place beneath; it is twice bless'd:
It blesseth him that gives, and him that takes."

Whilst admitting all this, I maintain that there is an unfortunate class—that of idiots—which has not hitherto received that share of attention to which it is entitled. Why is this? Is it due to a pampered selfishness which has chosen to draw a curtain of indifference around this unfortunate branch of the human race? Is the fountain of charity frozen up in East Anglia? Nothing of the kind, and I think this apparent neglect is mainly due to a misconception as to the nature of idiocy, and as to the amount of amelioration of which the subjects of this unfortunate infirmity are susceptible. It is with the view of removing this erroneous impression, that I have been requested to say a few words to you about idiocy, from a scientific point of view, my desire being to instruct the mind of the public as to the nature and character of the evil to be contended with, as to the probability of alleviating it, and as to the means best adapted to the attainment of this object.

In the few remarks that I shall make, I hope to show you that the study of idiocy is fraught with interest, not only to the man of science and the philanthropist, but to the political economist, the statesman, and the theologian. If it be asked what possible connection there can be between theology and idiocy, I would say, that if time permitted, I could show that the study of the nature and attributes of the idiot has a striking bearing on the much-disputed question of the connection between matter and mind, and also that it points to a conclusion directly opposed to the materialistic tendencies of the day.

DEFINITION OF IDIOCY.

Great confusion exists in the public mind as to the nature of idiocy. What is an idiot? Dr. Séguin, a celebrated writer on this subject, has described idiocy as a "specific infirmity of the cerebro-spinal centre," a definition which I need not say applies to a variety of infirmities to which flesh is heir, and such a definition only serves as a cloak for ignorance. Shakespeare, that wonderfully accurate observer of human nature, in several of his dramas has given a very good description of the acts of the idiot, who, he says, is "one who holds his bauble for his God;" and again, as "one who tells a tale full of sound and fury, signifying nothing." But neither he nor the psychologists of his day knew enough of the natural history of the idiot to attempt a logical definition.

As I have spent a great deal of time in the investigation of obscure points of cerebral pathology, of course the question of the idiot has not escaped my attention, and I submit the following definition:—

An idiot is a human being who possesses the tripartite nature of man— body, soul, and spirit, σωμα, ψυχη, πνευμα, but who is the subject of an infirmity consisting, anatomically, of a defective organisation and want of development of the brain, resulting in an inability, more or less complete, for the exercise of the intellectual, moral, and sensitive faculties. There are various shades and degrees of this want of development, from those whose mental and bodily deficiencies differ but slightly from the lowest of the so-called sound-minded, to those individuals who simply vegetate, and whose deficiencies are so decided as to isolate them, as it were, from the rest of nature.

Dr. Langdon Down[1] divides Idiocy into three primary groups: Congenital, Developmental, and Accidental. The Congenital includes all cases which at the period of birth manifest signs of the defective mental power. The Developmental group includes cases where the child manifests an average intelligence through infancy, but he is born with a proclivity to a mental break-down during one of the developmental crises, such as the first dentition, the second dentition, and puberty; the brain and nervous power are sufficient for their early years, but are insufficient to carry them through evolutional stages. The Accidental group includes cases where the child has been born with a normal nervous system, when unfortunately a fall, a fright, epilepsy, or some other cause may lead to a mental break-down, not of a genetic, but of a purely accidental origin. The various forms of idiocy are described in minute detail by Dr. Ireland,[2] to whose classical work I would refer those who may desire further information on this subject.

The first idiot that attracted the attention of scientific men was looked upon as a savage man, and every treatise on the subject contains some allusion to the so-called savage of the Aveyron, who excited so much curiosity, speculation, and interest among the psychologists of Paris in the early part of the present century.

In old books on medical nomenclature idiocy was classed amongst the varieties of insanity, and the visitor to a lunatic asylum half a century ago, would find the idiot skulking in the corner of a courtyard chained to a staple, and lying on a litter of straw; in fact, he was considered and treated more like a wild beast than a human being. He had but little talent given, and by neglect or abuse that little was lost; until, growing more and more brutal, he sank unregitting and unregretted into an early grave, without ever being counted as a man. Now, idiocy is not a form of insanity, and it is most important that no confusion should exist in the public mind upon this point, as the association of idiots and insane patients in the same asylum is a positive disadvantage to both classes. It is always a painful thing to see idiot children, whose mental faculties and physical powers, as I shall presently show, are capable of much development and improvement, wandering, without object or special care, about the wards of a Lunatic Asylum. They cannot receive there the training and supervision they specially require, and they often seriously interfere with the comfort of the other inmates, and meet in return, with ridicule and unkindness; moreover, their presence is a serious obstacle to the complete recovery of convalescent lunatics. I desire especially to press this point upon the legislators of the country, and, as in this county, our union houses are far too large for the requirements of the age, I would suggest that one or more of them might, with advantage, be devoted to the care and treatment of pauper idiots.[3]

Insanity is a loss more or less complete of faculties formerly possessed, it consists of a perturbation of the mental faculties after their complete development, it begins with average intelligence which gradually diminishes; whereas idiocy begins with a low amount of intelligence, which, in many instances, gradually increases; the difference has been thus beautifully described by a French psychologist, "L'homme en démence est privé des biens dont il jouissait autrefois, c'est un riche devenu pauvre. L'idiot a toujours été dans l'infortune et la misère." (The man that is mad is deprived of possessions which he formerly enjoyed, it is a rich man become poor; whereas the idiot has always been in misfortune and misery.) The distinction between the idiot and the insane is clear and marked. The madman suffers from abnormal development of brain, the idiot from an ill-developed brain—the mind of the madman is not in proper balance, in the idiot it is not in proper power.

The poor idiot (the word being derived from the Greek ισιοτης[4]) is alone in the world; isolated as it were from the rest of nature, he sees but does not perceive, he hears but does not understand or appreciate; the organs of sight and hearing may be perfect and yet useless; the impressions formed upon the optic and auditory nerves are duly transmitted to the sensorium, but no idea is there excited; he cares for nothing, and is alike indifferent to the grandeur as to the beauties of Nature; he stands unmoved at the thunder clap, the foam of the rushing cataract, or the roar of the mighty ocean; he heeds not the hum of the insect world or the song of the early lark, that winged chorister of the air; the star-bejewelled canopy of heaven, the mountain landscape lighted up with all the purple splendour of the setting sun, all these are nothing to him—he is a soul shut up in imperfect organs.

CAUSES OF IDIOCY.

It will be utterly impossible in the short time allotted to me, to enter at any length upon the various causes of idiocy, a study of which is, however, fraught with many a useful lesson. Suffice it to say that as the cause is always antecedent to any personal history of the child, idiocy is never dependent on the idiot himself, who has never become so through any vices of his own; he being in many instances the feeble expression of parental defects, and sometimes of parental vices, and is therefore more an object for commiseration than certain lunatics, who, in many instances, have become so through faults of their own. As to the social aspect of idiocy, it recognises no distinction of rank; it may occur in the homes of the affluent, or in the hovels of the most indigent. It is found in all civilised countries, but it is not an evil necessarily inherent in society, and is the result of the violation of natural laws, in some way or other, and at some time or other, and the effect may not show itself for two or three generations. A very large class of persons ignore the conditions upon which health and reason can co-exist; they pervert the natural appetites of the body, and the natural emotions of the mind, and thus bring down the awful consequences of their own ignorance upon the heads of their unoffending children.

Idiocy may be a congenital infirmity, or may be developed in early infancy. In the first category, the cause must necessarily be traced to intra-uterine life, and must be sought for in the history of the parents; in the second class, the cause may sometimes depend upon parental defects, and sometimes is due to a cerebral affection occurring soon after birth, but even in this class of cases, hereditary predisposition must be considered as a powerful factor in the genesis of the disease. In fact, the development of idiocy, whether congenital or otherwise, is in most instances to be attributed to an hereditary morbid vice, and it is one of the most common and striking forms of the degeneration of the human species.

Hereditary tendencies have much to do with the development of physical defects and bodily ailments, and this result is especially apparent in diseases of the nervous system; and there can be no doubt that heredity is a potent factor in the production of idiocy. Dr. Ireland says, "idiocy is, of all mental derangements, the most frequently propagated by descent;" and the statistics of Ludwig Dahl, of Christiana, showed that fifty per cent. of idiots had insane relations, those of Dr. Fletcher Beach showed a history of hereditary predisposition in 76 per cent., whilst those of Moreau, of Tours, give a proportion as high as 90 per cent.

In thus expressing myself, I should be sorry that my remarks should be construed as intended to cast any imputation upon those who have unfortunately an idiot in their family; the cause of the evil may be in some remote progenitor, for the transmission of the infirmity is not always direct, and the neurotic tendency may skip a generation, or be traced even further back.

Intemperance. One of the most fruitful causes of idiocy is the abuse— mark, I do not say the proper use—of alcoholic stimulants, which tends to bring families into a low and feeble condition, which thus becomes a prolific cause of idiocy in their children. From a report on idiocy, by Dr. Howe and other Commissioners appointed by the Governor of Massachusetts to ascertain the causes of this calamity in that State, it is stated that "out of 359 idiots, the condition of whose progenitors was ascertained, 99 were the children of inveterate drunkards;" and the report goes on to say further, "that when the parents were not actually habitual drunkards, yet amongst the idiots of the lower class, not one quarter of the parents could be considered as temperate persons. From a table drawn up by the late Dr. Kerlin, an American physician, in which the causes of the infirmity are given in 100 cases of idiotic children, I observe that in 38 of the number, intemperance on the part of the parents is traced as an accessory, main, direct, or indirect cause.

At the annual meeting of the British Medical Association, held at Cambridge, Dr. Fletcher Beach read a paper on the Intemperance of Parents as a predisposing cause of idiocy in children. In 430 patients, he was enabled to trace a history of parental intemperance in 138 cases, or 31·6 per cent.; of this number, 72 were males and 66 females."[5]

Other observers lay less stress upon parental intemperance as a cause of idiocy. Dr. Wilbur found that out of 365 cases in the State of Illinois, only eight cases were assigned to the abuse of drink in the parents; and Dr. Shuttleworth could trace this cause in only 16·38 per cent. of the cases observed by himself and by Dr. Fletcher Beach;[6] the same writer, under the head of toxic idiocy, mentions the case of an idiot boy, who was said to have been brought up on porter instead of milk. It will therefore be seen that there exists a great difference of opinion about the influence of intemperance of the parent in the causation of idiocy; but although statistics may vary upon this point, there cannot be a doubt that the children of drunken parents inherit an unhealthy nervous system, which in many cases culminates in idiocy.

Idiocy is especially prevalent in Norway, and Ludwig Dahl, a Norwegian writer, says that to the abuse of brandy, especially in the fathers, but also in the mothers during pregnancy, may be assigned an important, perhaps the most important, influence in the production of the large number of idiots in that country.

In considering this question, we must bear in mind that intemperance is only a relative term; for in the early part of the century we read of our ancestors indulging in a bottle of port wine to each individual, without, it seems, incurring the charge of drunkenness. There cannot be a doubt, however, that the habitual use of alcohol, without being carried to the extent of actual intoxication, is calculated to cause a low and feeble condition of the body, and thus conduce to the production of idiocy in the offspring; for we may fairly assume that what too severely tries the nervous system in one generation will appear in their descendants.[7] Without, therefore, exaggerating the influence of alcohol on the genesis of idiocy, I think I shall not be deviating from the path of strict scientific accuracy, if I say that over indulgence in alcoholic beverages is calculated to produce a low state of vitality, and a degeneration of nerve tissue which may culminate in the development of idiocy in subsequent generations.[8]

Just now that the attention of the Legislature is being prominently called to the treatment of habitual drunkards, it cannot be too widely known that their innocent offspring are but too frequently the victims of the brutish excesses of their parents, who, a few years ago, were well described by the then Secretary of State for the Home Department, when receiving a deputation on the subject, as not quite criminals nor quite lunatics, although nearly approaching both classes in many cases. The above statistics fully corroborate the pertinency of Lord Cross's remarks.

I do not allude to these facts with the view of casting any reflection upon the poor, honest, and temperate East Anglian labourer, who may be afflicted with the calamity of having an idiot child; but I merely mention them in order that they may serve as an additional caution against habits of intemperance, and may strengthen the hands of that noble band of philanthropists who are endeavouring to check the torrent of this hideous vice so prevalent in the present day.

Consanguine Marriages. There is no point connected with the causation of idiocy that has given rise to so much controversy as the marriage of near relations; formerly one of the most popular notions was that consanguineous marriages were among the most common causes of idiocy, whereas the researches of later observers have tended to modify, to a considerable extent, this sweeping assertion.

Different observers have furnished different results, as to the proportion of idiots found to be the offspring of consanguine marriages; thus Dr. Grabham's statistics give the proportion as about 2 per cent., Dr. Langdon Down's rather more than 5 per cent., and Dr. Shuttleworth's less than 5 per cent. The statistics of the Eastern Counties' Asylum, kindly supplied to me by Mr. Turner, the Resident Superintendent, show that about 6·5 per cent. were the offspring of cousins.

Of 359 cases observed by Dr. Howe, 17 were known to be the children of parents nearly related in blood. The history of these 17 families, the heads of which being blood relatives intermarried, showed that there were other causes to increase the chances of an infirm offspring, besides that of intermarriages, as most of the parents were intemperate or scrofulous; some were both the one and the other. There were born unto them 95 children, of whom 44 were idiotic, 12 others were scrofulous and puny, one was deaf, and one was a dwarf! In one family of 8 children, 5 were idiotic.[9]

Dr. Ireland, who has investigated this point with great minuteness, pertinently remarks that it has been the custom to collect instances of cousins who have married, and have had unhealthy children, as if this never happened to anyone else; and he adds that "the proper way to examine the question clearly, is to find what is the proportion of marriages of blood relations in a given population, and then to inquire if there be in the issue of such marriages a larger percentage of insane, idiotic, or otherwise unhealthy children."[10]

There cannot be a doubt that consanguinity has hitherto been considered too great a factor in the production of idiocy, and that in weighing the evidence, we must not lose sight of the fact that in many cases recorded, other factors beside inter[35]marriage of relatives have contributed concurrently to the development of the mental defect.[11]

Educational Overpressure. There is one cause of idiocy which has been pointed out by Dr. Séguin, and which he says is due to the unsatisfactory social conditions under which women of the present day exist. "As soon," he says, "as women assumed the anxieties pertaining to both sexes, they gave birth to children whose like had hardly been met with thirty years ago."[12]

Great prominence has lately been given to this subject by an oration on "Sex in Education," by Sir James Crichton Browne, at the Medical Society of London, in which he called attention to the "growing tendency to ignore intellectual distinctions between the sexes, to assimilate the education of girls to that of boys, and to throw men and women into industrial competition in every walk of life." Elsewhere, he adds, that "to throw women into competition with men is to insure to them a largely increased liability to organic nervous disease.... Woe betide the generation that springs from mothers amongst whom gross nervous degenerations abound." Sir J.C. Browne supports his views by showing that there are organic cerebral differences between men and women, and that therefore they must be educated in different ways, being destined to play different parts on the stage of human life.[13]

The above views of Sir J.C. Browne have not remained unchallenged, and the eminent psychologist has found uncompromising opponents in Mrs. Garrett Anderson and others, who stoutly refuse to recognise the position of the "Tacens et placens uxor" of old-time dreams. Mrs. Anderson, who, I need scarcely add, writes most temperately upon this matter, in alluding to Sir J.C. Browne's assumption of the intellectual difference between men and women, remarks, "All I would venture to say is that, if it could be proved that an average man differs from an average woman as much as Newton differed from a cretin, it would still be well to give the cretin all the training which he was capable of receiving.... When we hear it said that women will cease to be womanly if they enter professions or occasionally vote in parliamentary elections, we think that those who conjure up these terrors should try to understand women better, and should rid themselves of the habit of being frightened about nothing."[14]

The limits of this essay will not permit me to dwell at any great length on the important question under consideration. There cannot be a doubt that the tendency of the present age is to encourage women to choose careers and to accept burdens unfitted for them. In thus expressing myself, I distinctly deprecate any hostility to the woman's movement of the present day, which rests on the claim for women for an open career; and I should be glad to see our universities ignore the ancient and exploded prejudices, which led to the long subjection of women to hardship and inequality. They ask for the same facilities as are enjoyed by men, and they have amply shown that they can compete with men in intellectual pursuits, and all they ask is to be allowed to compete on equal terms. I therefore cordially welcome the gradual emancipation of women from comparative subjection to comparative freedom; but the multifarious fields of energy and usefulness open to modern women, have brought with them disadvantages as well as gains.

Whilst, therefore, unreservedly admitting the claims of the fin de siècle woman to freedom of action and to intellectual equality, I must think there are certain branches of study, described by a modern writer as belonging to the "gynagogue" class, which are less suited to women than some others; and amongst these, I would name the abstruse study of mathematics, for although success in this branch of knowledge may lead to a brilliant career as a high wrangler, I think that a female mathematical athlete is not suited for the duties and responsibilities of maternity, and that the mental endowments of her children are likely to be below the average.

I am quite aware that I am treading on dangerous and delicate ground, but although I would not discourage the highest aspirations of women, whether of an intellectual, social, or æsthetic character, I must think that a word of caution is necessary against the overpressure of the present day in the direction above indicated.[15] With every desire to treat this question from a liberal point of view, I desire to emphasise the fact that men and women have different parts to play on the stage of life, and should be trained differently; but provided mental overpressure is guarded against, I have no fear of women engaging in certain occupations which custom has not hitherto recognised as feminine, and experience has shown us that they may be safely left to follow the promptings of their own powers and instincts.

Amongst the various other predispositions to idiocy, I would mention scrofula, which, according to Dr. Ireland, is the remote cause of two-thirds of all cases; phthisis and epilepsy in the parents are also potent factors in the development of idiocy in their offspring.

Before quitting the question of the cause of idiocy, I should like to say a word or two about what is technically called its histology and its pathological anatomy. What is there in the brain that makes one man a senior wrangler and another an idiot? What is it that unfits one person for the discharge of the ordinary duties of domestic and social life, and endows another with capacities adapted for a statesman, a mathematician, or a philosopher? Is it a defect in the quantity or in the quality of the nervous matter of the brain? Does it depend on a malformation of the cranium, on the size or shape of the head? does the form of a cranium illustrate the quality of the mind whose cerebral substratum it encloses, or can genius of a high order enshrine itself in a comparatively narrow and malconstructed tenement?[16] Does mental capacity depend on the size or weight of the brain, or on the degree of complexity of the cerebral convolutions, or on their symmetry in each hemisphere?[17] Upon this point, I am bound to tell you that science speaks with a somewhat uncertain sound, volumes having been written upon it without any definite solution or tangible result.

An eminent Italian psychologist, Dr. Mingazzini, in a recent work on the study of the cerebral convolutions, shows that in men of genius, the brain offers no certain indications of intellectual eminence, either by the greater richness of the frontal or the parietal lobes; and in support of this opinion he cites the researches of Wagner, which showed that, in the development and richness of the convolutions, the brains of many celebrated Gottingen professors were inferior to those belonging to individuals of low intellectual capacity.[18]

The average brain weight in man may be said to range from 40 to 52½ ounces, and in women from 35 to 37½ ounces; the question of the increase in size and weight of the brain, in proportion to intellectual power, is by no means determined; statistics exist of the weight of 23 eminent men, the list being headed by Cuvier, the naturalist, whose brain weighed 64½ ounces, whilst that of the orator, Gambetta, weighed only 39 ounces, being much below the average weight in the adult male; an imbecile died at the Montrose Asylum, whose brain weighed 63 ounces, and the heaviest brain on record, which weighed 67 ounces, was that of a bricklayer, who could neither read nor write; it must therefore be conceded that no definite statement can be made as to the relation that brain weight has to intelligence.[19]

It was formerly supposed that idiots always presented some obvious malformation of the cranium or skull. This is by no means necessarily the case; one of the most remarkable cases of idiocy that has come under my notice was that of a child with a well-formed head, remarkably handsome face, and a well-proportioned body.

Dr. Ireland says, "the principal anomalies met with in the skull of genetic idiots are flatness of the head behind, a rapid slope of the clivus, an osseous rim round the foramen magnum, unsymmetrical size of the cavities on each side, irregularities in the wings of the sphenoid, and differences in the size and shape of the jugular and other foramina; but these appearances are not constant, and often the skull is quite regular, both in structure and capacity."[20]

One of the most noted writers on the subject, after stating that a number of scientific men had spent thirty years in measuring and weighing the heads of idiots, sums up their conclusions as follows:—

1st. There is no constant relation between the development of the cranium and the degree of intelligence.

2nd. The dimensions of the anterior part of the cranium, and especially of the forehead, are, at least, as great among idiots as others.[21]

3rd. Three-fifths of idiots have larger heads than men of ordinary intelligence.

4th. There is no constant relation between the degree of intelligence and the weight of the brain.[22]

5th. Sometimes the brain of idiots presents no deviation in form, colour, and density from the normal standard; it is, in fact, perfectly normal.

After such a statement as this, I can readily imagine that some of you may say, it seems to us that you doctors really know but little about the genesis of idiocy. I am afraid this is, to some extent, true. We are only on the threshold of inquiry, and science of to-day is unable to bridge over the gulf that separates matter from mind.

Modern investigation, however, does not quite bear out the above sweeping statements in their integrity, although the most conflicting theories have been enunciated. Doubtless, attention has been too much concentrated on the gross morphology of the brain, without taking into account microscopical appearances. Dr. Shuttleworth, in giving the result of his long experience at the Royal Albert Asylum says, "We have occasionally found, when least expected, extraordinary defects in brain conformation;... microscopic examination will discover in many instances some abnormality of structure, such as the preponderance of simply formed braincells devoid of processes, denoting persistence of foetal structures; or, on the other hand, degenerative changes resulting from inflammatory atrophy."[23]

Professor Luys, of Paris,[24] gives the result of the examination of the brain of 14 idiots, the anomalies observed being want of symmetry in the frontal lobes, and partial atrophy of the cortical folds especially of the frontal convolutions.[25]

Quite recently, Dr. Andriessen, at a meeting of the Leeds and West Riding Medico-Chirurgical Society, exhibited specimens of the brains of epileptic idiots, which showed conditions of microgyria with atrophy and sclerosis of the convolutions.

In considering the pathology of idiocy, I think sufficient attention has not been given to the chemical constitution of the cerebral substance. The most extravagant notions were at one time prevalent as to the rôle played by phosphorus in the animal economy; the Dutch naturalist, Moleschott, maintaining that "without phosphorus there was no thought." A celebrated chemist, Couerbe, also considered phosphorus to be the exciting principle of the brain, and according to him, the brain of ordinary men contained 2½ per cent. of phosphorus, that of the idiot 1½, and that of the madman 4 to 4½; from these data he concluded, "that the absence of phosphorus in the brain reduced man to the condition of the brute; that a great excess of this element irritated the nervous system and plunged the individual into the frightful delirium which we call madness; and that a medium proportion re-established the equilibrium and produced the admirable harmony which is none else than the soul of the spiritualists."[26] Professor Janet, in criticising the above theory, remarks that the brain of fishes, who do not pass for great thinkers, contains a large amount of phosphorus, also that the statistics of M. Lassaigne have shown that the brain of madmen does not contain more phosphorus than that of sane individuals.[27]

The late Bishop of Carlisle, in rebutting this phosphorus theory, remarks,

"Why should we not go further and assert that there could be no thought without carbon or without any other element of which the human body is composed; for you can have no actual thought without a living creature, and no living creature without a body, and no body without carbon."[28]

I have treated the subject of the Chemistry of the Brain at considerable length in my treatise on "Aphasia and the Localisation of Articulate Language," to which book I would refer those who desire further information in reference to the connection between the amount of phosphorus and intellectual vigour.

MATTER AND MIND.

"Quare frustra sudaverit, qui cœlestia religionis arcana nostræ rationi adaptare conabitur." Bacon, "De Augmentis Scientiarum."

I have already stated that the study of idiocy was of great interest to the theologian, for I can imagine no more powerful weapon for combating the materialistic tendencies of the day than is furnished by a consideration of the natural history of the idiot. This is neither the time nor the place for me to enter into the question of the mysterious connection between matter and mind, a subject which I have developed at some length in my published works.[29] In my various public appeals on behalf of the Asylum for Idiots, I have also usually taken the opportunity of pointing out how the experience afforded by the study of idiocy is utterly opposed to the extravagant dogmas of the materialistic school, and to the crude notions which pseudo-science has engendered; and I have also shown how the results of idiot training furnish a forcible demonstration of the dualistic theory of mind and matter, upon which science reposed till the times of Spinosa, Laplace, Haeckel, Huxley, and others.

The pseudo-philosophers of our time have bewildered the public mind by the wild flights of their imagination; thought, the so-called spiritual attributes of man, are merely a function of brain protoplasm; the brain, say they, secretes thought, just as the liver secretes bile, or as oxygen and sulphur produce sulphuric acid, and all the varied phenomena of nature are nothing more than the molecular changes of matter; the operations of the mind are but the products of the caudate cells of the brain, and volition and consciousness are mere physical manifestations. They see only the physio-chemical side of nature, they utterly ignore any spiritual attribute in man, they regard metaphysics as a relic of mediæval superstition, and they assert that all mental operations are bodily functions, and simply the result of some molecular or atomic change in the brain; indeed, the German philosophers go so far as to say that life itself is only a "special and most complicated act of mechanics;"[30] that there is no real distinction between living and dead matter, and that vitality is a metaphysical ghost (ein metaphysisches Gespenst).[31]

At the International Psychological Congress held in Paris, in 1878, at which it was my privilege to be present, Professor Mierzejewski, of St. Petersburg, laid before the congress the result of his elaborate experiments on the brains of idiots, his communication being illustrated by casts of the brains of idiots, and also of certain animals, and the learned Russian professor's conclusions strongly militated against the theories of the philosophers of whom I have been speaking.

In order to understand the great value and import of Dr. Mierzejewski's investigations, I must remind you that the human brain is composed of two kinds of nerve structure, of an essentially different nature, grey matter and white matter. Examined microscopically, the grey matter is found to be composed of cells, while the white matter consists of fibres; their function also is different, the former being regarded as the generator of nerve force, while the latter simply serves as the medium by which this force is transmitted. As the manifestation of the intellectual powers is supposed to be in some way connected with the development of the grey matter of the cerebral convolutions, one would expect to find in idiots a deficiency of this element of brain tissue.[32] Dr. Mierzejewski maintained that this is by no means the case, and he mentioned an instance of an idiot in whose brain the surface of grey matter was enormous. So it would seem that there is no fixed relation between the amount of grey matter of the brain and intellectual power, for richness of grey substance and abundance of nerve cells may be accompanied by idiocy.

Now, as these startling statements of the Russian professor were not made in a hole and corner, but were enunciated in the presence of leading psychologists from all parts of the world, I felt myself justified in telling the materialists that they must be faced, and either answered or admitted as correct; and as my comments upon these experiments were subsequently published in a leading London periodical and widely circulated, I am now justified in assuming that the inferences I then drew from these remarkable experiments cannot be controverted, and that the time has not yet arrived when the broad distinctions between mind and matter are to be obliterated, and man reduced to a mere automaton, a creature of a blind necessity.

Without unduly exaggerating the importance of Dr. Mierzejewski's experiments, it must be admitted that very great interest attaches to them at this juncture, when attention is so widely directed to the mysterious connection between matter and mind. Unhappily, instead of solving the question, the Russian professor's researches tend to shroud it in a still deeper mystery, and show that what has been termed the "slippery force of thought—the vis vivida animæ"—cannot be weighed in the balance; and they fully justify the eloquent language of a recent writer when he says, "Far more transcendent than all the glories of the universe is the mind of man. Mind is indeed an enigma, the solution of which is apparently beyond the reach of this very mind, itself the problem, the demonstrator, the demonstration, and the demonstrants ."

Those who maintain that the brain is the organ of the mind, do not tell us what we are to understand by organ, brain, or mind; they seem to me to confound two things, the one with the other. In fact, they make no distinction between thought, mind, consciousness, and the instrument by which these attributes become externally manifested. It is true, we have no evidence to show that the mind can operate independently of the nervous system; on the contrary, all physiological data bearing upon the question of this mutual relation, go to prove that where there is no nervous system there are no mental manifestations. Moreover, as G.H. Lewes says, "It is the man, and not the brain, that thinks: it is the organism as a whole, and not one organ, that feels and acts."[33]

Every faculty manifests itself by means of matter, but it is important not to confound the faculty with the corporeal organ upon which the external manifestation of such faculty depends. The word organ is the name given to a part of the human frame by which we have sensation, and by means of which we do a certain act or work; such are the organs of sight, sound, smell, taste, and touch. All these organs are passive, and require to be operated on ab extra, precisely in the same way as the musical organ, which is an instrument constructed by man, requires man's interference for the production of musical sounds.

When a musician sits down to a piano, the music cannot be said to be in the instrument, but in the soul of the performer. If the instrument be in good order, the inspiration of a Thalberg or of a Liszt will become apparent; break the cords or otherwise damage the instrument, and nothing but discordant strains are produced, the musical faculty of the performer, however, remaining unaffected. We are all familiar with Plato's celebrated dialogue on the Immortality of the Soul, where a disputant with Socrates inquires if the soul is not like the harmony of a lyre, more beautiful, more divine than the lyre itself, but yet is nothing without the lyre, vanishing when this instrument is broken.

Let me further illustrate this point by an allusion to the electric telegraph, by means of which ideas and words are transmitted from mind to mind with a rapidity to which ordinary language cannot attain. Now, the electrical battery may be not inaptly compared to the brain, and the telegraph wires to the nerves which emanate from it. If the battery be out of order, or the telegraph wires be broken, this lightning language, by which mind speaks to mind, becomes impossible. In the same way, idiocy may be considered as a disease of the instrument rather than of the performer; the idiot's brain is damaged and has become an unfit instrument for the outward manifestation of the powers of the mind, but the lowest idiot possesses the germs of intellectual activity and moral responsibility; and within his malconstructed organism, there lies concealed in its fragile, fleshly casket, a precious jewel of immortality—an imperishable essence that is destined to live on for ever and for aye, through countless æons of time, when the dicta of these dreamers of whom I have been speaking, to use the language of one of them, "shall have melted away like streaks of morning cloud into the infinite azure of the past."

I repeat it, we must take care not to confound the organ with the person who possesses this organ: the eye is not that which sees, it is only the organ by which we see; the ear is not that which hears, it is only the organ by which we hear. Precisely in the same way and in the same sense, the brain is the organ of mind, the organ by which our mental faculties become externally manifested. That it cannot be otherwise is shewn by the results of memory. The brain is of a perishable nature, its atoms are constantly changing; the body is continually throwing off old particles and appropriating new ones, every breath that is drawn, and every exertion that is made, cause some minute change in the bodily frame-work, so that it is never entirely the same;[34] there is no person, therefore, who has the same brain that he had 20 years ago; and the vivid impressions of the past are utterly inexplicable on the supposition that mental activity is a mere function of any perishable organ like the brain, but they necessitate the conclusion that mind and body, spirit and matter, are two entirely heterogeneous substances, and that mind—the concrete Ego—is independent of the material organ by which its external manifestation is alone possible.[35]

However tempting it might be, I feel I must not trespass any further by dwelling on the mysterious connection between matter and mind, a subject the complete comprehension of which is beyond the limits of our finite capacities. As Goethe philosophically remarks, "We are eternally in contact with problems. Man is an obscure being, he knows little of the world, and of himself least of all."

It would seem that the great Roman orator, nearly 2,000 years ago, with prescient eye, foresaw the attempts that would hereafter be made to pry into the hidden mysteries of Nature, when he said:—

"Latent ista omnia, Luculle, crassis occultata et circumfusa tenebris, ut nulla acies humani ingenii tanta sit, quæ penetrare in cœlum, terra intrare possit."

These lines of Cicero would seem to be peculiarly applicable to certain modern philosophers, who, in their attempts to bridge over the gulf—the impassable gulf—which separates matter from mind, persistently ignore the fact that there are certain things which, from their very nature, are beyond the pale of precise knowledge, and which cannot be determined by physical investigation—which, in fact, lie outside the sphere of man's intellect. I believe the question I am discussing is one of these, and that, although we may grope with the taper of science into the dark caverns whence seem to issue the springs of humanity, we shall probably fail to understand the mysterious connection between matter and mind, a theme essentially beyond the grasp of human intelligence, and which cannot be fathomed by the puny plummet of human thought or touch.

The study of the idiot is calculated to elucidate this overwhelmingly important subject, and I believe the Idiot Asylum is destined to become the arena and battlefield on which this great question will have to be fought out.

THE PNEUMA, OR SPIRITUAL ATTRIBUTE OF THE IDIOT.

Ὁ δε νους εοικεν εγγινεθαι ουσια

τις ουσα, και ου φθειρεσθαι.

Aristot. De Anima, I. 4.

Inasmuch as the instrument by which the manifestation of mind is alone possible is undoubtedly damaged in idiots, they were formerly supposed not to belong to the human family, and their place in the order of creation was disputed. All admitted that they had the σωμα, or material part of our nature; they also conceded to them the ψυχη, or principle of animal life, but they considered that the πνευμα, or spirit of immortal life—that which essentially differentiates man from the brute—was absent in the idiot. This idea seemed to have been entertained by a great theologian of the 16th century, who, on being asked by a father what he was to do with his idiot boy, replied that the child might be drowned as he possessed no soul! Times are happily changed. We don't admit the lawfulness of drowning idiots in these days, but we teach them to swim against the adverse currents to which they are exposed; we buoy them up on the tempestuous waves of life; we pilot them through the rocks and shoals of their ill-starred career till their chequered race is run, and they are safely landed in the haven of everlasting rest.

Not only in the 16th century, but certain philosophers of a later date have questioned the idiot's place in creation, and have disputed his right to be classed among the human family; and some scientists—believers in the so-called doctrine of Evolution, as applied to the Descent of Man—have gone so far as to pretend that the brain of the microcephalic idiot is so far removed from the human type, as to constitute him a connecting link between man and the anthropoid apes! Now, the interesting results of our training institutions, showing the capacity for progressive improvement which exists in the idiot, gives the lie to this absurd and purely sensational hypothesis.

Here let me add that I strongly deprecate introducing the odium theologicum into the discussion of this subject, being fully conscious of the futility of attempting to check an unwelcome or distasteful theory by means of ecclesiastical censures; and I further admit that in anything like a scientific demonstration of truth, an appeal to the affections would be absurdly out of place.[36] Moreover, I should not reject the Darwinian theory from any sensational notion that its adoption was derogatory to Man's dignity, and I fully echo the sentiment of the naturalist who said that he would prefer being descended from a good honest monkey, than to be obliged to avow himself the offspring of certain fanatical enemies of scientific knowledge and progress; but I do complain of the tendency of the present day to accept new ideas without knowing or caring how to sift them. Everything is hypothetical, and allowed to enter the mind through the ivory gate of fancy; and on purely hypothetical premises, an attempt is made to found conclusive arguments. Strip the assertions of all their vagueness and superficial varnish, and reduce them to a skeleton of logical statement, and we shall see how much is assumed and how little is proved; and we shall find that we are asked to accept a chain of hypotheses, as if it were an induction founded on ascertained and indisputable facts. In thus expressing myself, I wish to add that the ultimate goal of the scientist is the establishment of truth, and I should as soon attempt to stop the progress of the avalanche that has become dislodged from the mountain top, as to try to bar the path of scientific progress, or to extinguish the torch of discovery. The tide of scientific truth will continue to flow on in spite of the modern Canutes, who may utter from time to time their imperial commands to stay its course. Magna est veritas et prevalebit.

The supporters of evolution base their arguments upon the remarkable resemblance between the brain of man and that of certain other animals. Now, I admit this striking analogy; I admit that every chief fissure and fold in the brain of man has its counterpart in that of the gorilla and the ourang-outang; and I am not prepared to deny the statement, that as far as the organ of intelligence is concerned, there is no very striking physical difference between him who weighs the stars and makes the light tell its secrets as to the constitution of distant worlds, and the howling senseless brute, who lives merely to satisfy his animal appetites. All animals of the vertebrate type are constructed on a plan which is essentially similar, not only as regards their skeleton, but as regards their brain. I don't deny that man is an animal, and that he has the essential properties of a highly organised one; but what I do maintain is, that the brain, after all, is merely an instrument by which the high psychological attributes peculiar to man become externally manifested.[37] Thought is not phosphorus, as some would have us believe; the human mind is not the result of a mere molecular arrangement of cerebral matter. There is something over and above all this, and the very resemblance of man's physical nature to that of some members of the brute creation, proves beyond all doubt that his superiority to them is hyperphysical, and I fully endorse Mr. Froude's philosophical remarks, when he says, "It is nothing to me how the Maker of me has been pleased to construct the organised substance which I call my body. It is mine, but it is not I. The νους, the intellectual spirit, being an ουσια—an essence—I believe to be an imperishable something which has been engendered in me from another source." The unhappy idiot, that stricken member of our race, possesses the tripartite nature of man—for he has not only the σωμα or material part, and the ψυχη or principle of animal life, but he also undoubtedly possesses the πνευμα or principle of immortal life.

The above statement could be amply borne out by a reference to cases which have been observed in idiot asylums. I will, however, mention but three:—An idiot boy has been known to retire alone, when there was a thunderstorm, to ask God to take care of his father, who was a sailor. A former superintendent of our Asylum, the late Mr. Millard, noticed one of the inmates praying in private, and on saying to the boy, "God hears prayer," he quietly observed, "Yes, and answers it, too." A little boy in the Massachussetts Asylum for Idiots was in declining health, and became, during his dying illness, an object of great interest to the matron and attendants. Unbidden, he said his prayers frequently, and putting up his little hand, he muttered, "Me want to go up! me want to go up!" Surely he was thinking of some sort of hereafter, because he added distinctly, "They'll say, here comes one of the boys from the Boston School for Idiots." The approach of death seemed to awaken his spiritual life; out of the decaying body appeared to rise the growing soul, for, after repeating the verse of a hymn, the spirit of this simple child became liberated from its earthly tenement—its material habitat—the connection between matter and mind was severed, and, to use the touching language of his biographer, "this poor little idiot boy bade a long adieu to his sorrowing friends, and doubtless there was then joy in heaven, as the recording angel wrote in the Book of Life the name of George Tobey."[38]

In an interesting essay published many years ago, entitled, "A Morning at Essex Hall, Colchester," its author, the Rev. Edwin Sidney, in describing his visit to the Asylum, remarked that, "The conduct of those who go to Church on Sunday is very decorous. One of the most cheering things in connection with these objects of benevolent solicitude, is the capability some of them manifest in receiving and being comforted by religion. There are amongst them instances of high conscientiousness and piety, which might be examples to such as are gifted with unimpaired faculties."

If any apology be due for pointing out how the mysterious connection between mind and matter may be illustrated by a study of idiocy, I will observe that the subject is of such absorbing interest that it is well that it should occasionally be removed from the heated arena of biological bias, into the calmer and more judicial atmosphere of the class of readers who may be interested in the important subject I am endeavouring to elucidate.

TREATMENT AND RESULTS.
"Distinguish'd link in being's endless chain,
Midway from nothing to the Deity.
Though sully'd and dishonour'd, still divine,
An heir of glory, a frail child of dust.
Helpless immortal!"—Young.

According to the census of 1881, there were about 32,717 idiots and imbeciles in England and Wales; the Census Commissioners, however, ascertained that owing to the reticence of parents, the returns were far from trustworthy, and, after careful inquiry, they estimated the total number of idiots and imbeciles at 41,940; of these, it is calculated that about 3,000 cases belong to the four Eastern Counties. Of this number, it is estimated that, after deducting pauper and other cases not considered suitable for this charity, there remain at least 1,000 idiots who need the benefits of the Eastern Counties' Asylum, whereas, our present accommodation is limited to 250 cases.[39]

The Board of Directors being forcibly impressed with their inability adequately to supply the wants of the district, have recently instituted a Permanent Endowment Fund. As the institution is mainly supported by voluntary contributions, the fluctuating nature of which has often caused considerable anxiety, the Board has felt the desirability of placing a considerable portion of their resources on a more solid basis; and it is with the view of giving stability and permanence to the work of the Asylum, that the Endowment Fund has been started, which it is proposed shall be inalienable, the interest only being used for the purposes of the Institution. In the year 1891, H.R.H. the Prince of Wales, with the view of furthering this object, graciously consented to preside at a Festival Dinner, at the Hotel Metropole, London, which resulted in an immediate contribution of £6,000. This fund, started under such happy auspices, has already reached the sum of £25,334 12s. 8d., which it is hoped may eventually reach £50,000, the amount which the Directors think indispensable to insure the efficient maintenance of the Asylum.

Now let us bring this matter home to ourselves. Where are the 3,000 unhappy blighted individuals that claim the Eastern Counties for their home? It is true that some of them are in the homes of the affluent, but the greater number are in the cottages of the poor, where the trouble of providing for one such member often reduces a working family to pauperism; the poor child beloved by its parents, is, perhaps, loathed by their neighbours, is avoided by other children, hidden from visitors, a constant care and sorrow to the mother, a source of anxious foresight to the father; in fact, the poor idiot child is like a Upas tree, that poisons the whole atmosphere around it, and the burden of his presence in a poor man's family is a new weight added to the load that was already sinking them down. Perhaps you may say, we agree with you, we lament as you do, that the narrow home of the humble artisan should be rendered intolerable by the presence of these stricken members of our race; but, we have been given to understand, that if not absolutely incurable, but very little can be done for them, that they baffle the efforts of the most zealous educators, and are almost beyond the reach of human sympathy.

Now this was the language generally used half a century ago, and a celebrated French authority on the subject, Esquirol, considered that idiots were what they must remain for the rest of their lives; that there was no possibility of ameliorating their condition, and that no means were known by which a larger amount of intelligence could be developed in them.[40] In fact, an effort to ameliorate the condition of the congenital imbecile was regarded by psychologists and physicians as absolutely hopeless, and the standard "Dictionnaire de Médecine," published in 1837, broadly stated that it was useless to attempt to combat idiotism; in order that the intellectual exercise might be established, it would be necessary to change the conformation of organs which are beyond the reach of all modification. So great was the pessimism prevalent on this subject, that it was insinuated that the idea of teaching an idiot could only enter the brain of one somewhat closely allied to that class!

Now, I am happy to tell you, that in the broad daylight of the nineteenth century, science gives an emphatic denial to this statement. Yes, the results obtained at our own Asylum and elsewhere, show that much, very much, may be done for the unhappy idiot, who in a private house is an intolerable incubus, but who, under proper training in a suitable asylum, becomes sociable, affectionate, and happy. It has been shown that in the majority of cases, the idiot may not only cease to be a source of annoyance and danger to those around him, but by care and training he may be made able to contribute to his own sustenance; the knowledge of simple trades of a mechanical kind, such as that of a carpenter, shoemaker, or tailor, has been reached by some, and household industrial pursuits have fitted others for domestic usefulness.

A celebrated German authority, Herr Saeger, of Berlin, has stated that in his establishment he had indubitable cases of idiocy, in which the head was small and malformed, yet in which the results of education were so triumphant, that they were ultimately able to mix with the world without being recognised as idiots. Further, he tells us that in one instance a young man underwent confirmation without the priest suspecting that he had been delivered from idiocy.

Dr. Shuttleworth records the case of an inmate of the Royal Albert Asylum, who became, under instruction, an expert joiner, and from being a very imp of mischief, grew up into a well-conducted, self-reliant youth, and ultimately emigrated to one of our colonies, and when he was last heard of, he was practising his trade in a leading city.[41]

Equally satisfactory results have been obtained in our own Asylum. A few years ago, a boy of eight was admitted into our Asylum, who was quite unmanageable at home, a terrible incubus in the household of which he formed part, and the constant subject of jeers and derisions on the part of the other juveniles of the village. After about six months' systematic training, one of the officials of the Asylum wrote to inform me that the boy had so much improved that he was afraid the Commissioners of Lunacy, at their next visit, would consider the boy no longer a fit subject for detention in the Asylum. Being on a short visit to his relatives, who reside near Norwich, he was brought to me for inspection, when I was struck with the miraculous transformation that had been effected; from a restless, destructive boy, he had been changed into a well-conducted lad, and he had actually been taught to write. At my request, he wrote very legibly his name and address, with the date, "James Smith, Colchester;" but he made a little mistake in the date, writing backwards, in the Chinese fashion—it being September 29th, he wrote "September 92nd!" This same boy was regularly employed as one of the gardeners to the institution, and has recently been discharged, and is now earning his own living as gardener in a private family. This case illustrates a peculiarity not infrequently remarked in the inmates of an idiot asylum, that is the remarkable propensity they have for imitation and shamming. This boy came to stay with his relatives in Norfolk for a few weeks, when every few days he would have an epileptic fit. When his holiday was over and he had returned to the Asylum, these fits recurred, and were, of course, reported to the medical attendant, who had a shrewd suspicion the boy was shamming. He thereupon said to the attendant: "The next time a fit comes on, I must apply a redhot iron to the soles of the feet, it will hurt him, but it will cure him." From that time the boy had no epileptic fits!

Thyroid Treatment of Idiocy.—My sketch of the treatment of Idiocy would be incomplete without an allusion to the injection or internal administration of a preparation of the thyroid gland of the sheep, a method of treatment brought into notoriety by Professors Kocher and Schiff, on the continent, and by Professor Victor Horsley, Dr. Murray, and others in this country. Numerous cases have been published claiming successful results, and the thyroid treatment has been spoken of as a cure for at least one of the forms of idiocy.

Without quite endorsing this sweeping and enthusiastic statement, there cannot be a doubt that this method opens up a hopeful vista in the treatment of idiocy; in fact, Dr. Ireland has furnished me with the particulars of a girl, aged five years, treated by thyroid juice, in whom "the improvement was so decided that it seemed an escape from idiocy into normal intelligence."[42]

A striking instance of the good results of thyroid treatment has lately occurred in the Eastern Counties' Asylum, the particulars of which have been kindly furnished to me by Mr. Kirkby, the Resident Medical Officer. Esther C., aged 19, was admitted Nov. 8th, 1894, with marked symptoms of Sporadic Cretinism. She was at once put on thyroid treatment, beginning with half a five-grain tabloid gradually increased to a tabloid once, twice, and sometimes three times a day, intermitting them for short periods. Latterly, she has been taking one tabloid a day. Under this treatment, she has gained 10 lbs. in weight, and has grown 5 inches; the features are not so coarse, the previous myxœdematous condition of the subcutaneous tissues has subsided, the outline of the features having become more defined, and the skin which was formerly dry and rough, has become soft and naturally moist, having lost a great deal of its puffiness; but the most obvious change in the patient is the disappearance of the two prominent elastic swellings (pseudo-lipomata) which formerly occupied the posterior triangle of the neck on each side. The mental condition has also improved, she takes more interest in amusements, and her voluntary movements are much more rapid. This patient is still under observation, and the results hitherto attained afford a favourable illustration of the beneficial effects of this mode of treatment.

At a meeting of the New York Academy of Medicine of March 12th, 1896, Dr. Emily Lewi reported the history of a very marked case of Cretinism in a girl, aged 13 months, who was put on thyroid treatment; improvement was noted in a week, and the child grew gradually intelligent. At this same meeting, Dr. G.M. Hammond expressed the opinion, that for thyroid treatment to be effectual, it must be begun in early life.[43]

My colleague, Dr. Burton-Fanning, has recently shown me a case of Cretinism under his care, at the Lind Infirmary for Children, in which thyroid treatment produced the most favourable results, not only of a physical, but of a psychical character. Although the child was four years old, he had not previously spoken a word, and understood nothing; but during the treatment, his expression became much less vacant, and the faculty of speech was roused into action.

Several valuable contributions have lately been made to our knowledge of the effects of thyroid feeding, more especially in the treatment of insanity, not however the less valuable as a guide to its probable benefit in idiocy. I wish more especially to allude to the researches of Dr. Lewis C. Bruce, at the Royal Asylum, Edinburgh, as reported in the "Journal of Mental Science" for January and October, 1895. There is much in the above essay that I could profitably comment upon, but I will content myself with saying that the outcome of these researches, which intimately concern the treatment of idiocy, is that Dr. Bruce has established the fact that thyroid feeding acts as a direct cerebral stimulant, which he thinks "may prove advantageous in cases where the higher cortical cells remain in an anergic condition." Dr. Bruce mentions the case of a patient who had not spoken for several months; one day, during the administration of the thyroid extract, he suddenly began to talk, and soon became quite communicative.

Whilst these pages are passing through the press, M. Auguste Voisin, Physician to La Salpêtrière, has had the courtesy to send me detailed particulars of a case of insanity in which the success of the thyroid treatment was phenomenal. The patient was a female, aged 25, and her mental derangement assumed the form of religious monomania, insomnia, and aural hallucinations; there was great emaciation, dryness of the skin, and cold extremities.[44]

No benefit having resulted from six months' treatment, including hypnotism, M. Voisin determined to try the subcutaneous injection of sterilised thyroid juice. After a few weeks of this treatment, a notable amelioration was observed; shortly afterwards all her unfavourable symptoms disappeared, and she was discharged cured.

One of the most interesting features in this case is the result of the analysis of the blood, as to its corpuscular richness. Before thyroid treatment was commenced, the number of corpuscles was only 2,225,000 per cubic millimetre; after the cure by the thyroid juice, the number was more than doubled, being 4,774,000 per cubic millimetre. In Dr. Lewis Bruce's cases, to which I have already referred, the result was the reverse of that observed by M. Voisin; for in the eight uncomplicated cases recorded by Dr. Bruce, with one exception, there was in all of them a diminution in the number of red corpuscles.

At the discussion on Myxœdema, at the Edinburgh Medico-Chirurgical Society, to which I have already alluded, Dr. Alexander Bruce showed a case of myxœdema under the care of Professor Fraser, in the Royal Infirmary, in which, as the result of thyroid feeding, a condition of relative anæmia had been developed. The patient had no murmurs when admitted, but since the administration of thyroid preparations, basal and mitral systolic bruits had developed themselves. It is further stated that the blood corpuscles had fallen from 4,600,000 to 3,700,000, and hæmoglobin from 78 per cent. to 59 per cent.[45]

Further researches would therefore seem to be necessary, before we can arrive at a satisfactory conclusion as to what effect the thyroid treatment has upon the blood.

Possibly the dose of the thyroid preparation may be an important factor in the result, for Dr. Byrom Bramwell, in an important and exhaustive monograph upon this subject, says, that anæmia is apt to be produced by large doses of the remedy; and he mentions a case where the red blood corpuscles and the hæmoglobin underwent a marked diminution during the period of acute thyroidism, but rapidly increased under the subsequent administration of small doses of the remedy.[46]

The subject of blood analysis is most important, as tending to throw some light upon a matter at present but little understood, namely the physiological effect of thyroid preparations upon the blood.

Dr. Telford-Smith has reported four cases of Sporadic Cretinism treated by thyroid extract at the Royal Albert Asylum, Lancaster, when a well-marked improvement was noticed in each case. The clinical history of these cases is given with minute detail by Dr. Telford-Smith, and is well worthy of close study by those interested in this subject.[47]

Quite recently, at the Annual Meeting of the British Medical Association, held at Carlisle in August of the present year, communications were read on the Thyroid Treatment of Cretinism and Imbecility, by Dr. Rushton Parker, Dr. Telford-Smith, Dr. John Thomson, and others. An animated discussion ensued, the tendency of which pointed to the undoubted advantages both physically and mentally of the use of this remedy.

Although the physiological effects of thyroid feeding may not be definitely recognised and understood, there is overwhelming evidence to show that it produces marked psychical results, that it acts as a direct cerebral stimulant, and we have every reason to rely upon it as a valuable adjuvant to our treatment of idiocy; and it is not too much to say that the treatment of this infirmity, as well as of other mental defects, by thyroid extract or some other preparation of the thyroid gland, is one of the greatest triumphs of modern medicine; but much still remains to be learnt, as Professor Victor Horsley remarks, "So definite and pronounced is the cachexia thyroidectomica, that few subjects in the range of pathology offer a more fruitful and inviting field of research."[48]

Craniectomy.—The operation of Craniectomy (that is the cutting of strips of bone from the cranium) has been recommended and practised in cases of microcephalic idiocy, an operation suggested upon the theory of premature synostosis, or closure of the cranial sutures, thus causing an arrest in the development of the subjacent cerebral tissue. Although I could not omit a reference to this operation, it has not met with general acceptance, and one of the most recent writers on this subject, M. Bourneville, physician at Bicêtre, discourages it altogether; and from his examination of the skulls of a number of idiots, he affirms that "in the immense majority of cases, there was no premature synostosis, and that neither normal anatomy, pathological anatomy, or physiology, justified the operation of Craniectomy."[49] The late Sir George Humphry was of the same opinion, as, after an examination of 19 microcephalic skulls, he said, "There is nothing to suggest that the deficiency in the development of the skull was the leading feature in the deformity, or anything to give encouragement to the practice lately adopted in some instances of a removal of a part of the bony case, with the idea of affording more space and freedom for the growth of the brain."[50]

At a recent meeting of the New York State Medical Society, Professor Dana read a paper on Craniectomy for Idiocy and Imbecility, and he gave the following result of 81 cases:—In 35, there was improvement; in 22, no improvement; and death ensued in 24 cases. The conclusion at which Professor Dana arrives is that "it is largely through its pedagogic influence that an improvement takes place, and that the operation is allied in its effect to a severe piece of castigation!" Dr. Dana freely admits that this view of craniectomy for idiocy and imbecility lends itself readily to humour, and it would seem that he intended to kill the operation by ridicule.[51]

Of course, Dr. Ireland has something to say upon this point, and after a brief review of the literature of the subject, he says: "So many cases have been collected of microcephales with open sutures, that it is not likely that anyone will continue to hold that the small size of the brain is owing to the sutures closing in, and thus hindering their growth. Even in those cases where the sutures have closed in before birth, the question still remains whether the brain ceased to grow because the sutures are closed, or whether the sutures closed in because the brain ceased to grow; or, lastly, whether both the brain and its coverings ceased to grow under a common cause."[52]

The benefits to be derived in apparently hopeless cases of idiocy, from the systematic and persevering use of all the modern adjuvants and appliances now available for treatment, are now so universally recognised, that it would be superfluous to dwell further on this point. Science has done much for the idiot, and she will do more, for her motto is "Excelsior," and her votaries are not content to linger with complacency on the heights already attained, but they look for the period when, by the powerful lever of an enlightened philanthropy, this benighted race shall be raised from the grovelling level of the brute, to the highest attainable pitch of bodily perfection.

I trust that I have said enough to justify an earnest appeal for sympathy with this unfortunate branch of the human family. I have endeavoured to show that a great social evil exists amongst us, and that duty and interest should alike concur to induce us to face this evil and to master it. I have endeavoured to point out how the care and training of the idiot has become one of the recognised obligations of a philanthropic public. At the Eastern Counties' Asylum, we are trying to mitigate as far as we can this great social calamity, and our efforts have hitherto been crowned with unlooked-for success. We are doing a grand and glorious work, and I ask you to come and help us; the Board of Directors, a noble band of philanthropists, who devote a considerable amount of time to the objects of this charity, ask you to come and help us; nay, more, from the cottage homes in East Anglia rendered miserable by the presence of these unhappy beings, a thousand

voices cry to you with trumpet tongue, "Come and help us."
We have in the Eastern Counties' Asylum an institution admirably adapted for the care and treatment of the idiot; standing in its own grounds of seven acres, it is furnished with all the machinery necessary to grapple with this great social calamity, and by the judicious combination of medical, physical, moral, and intellectual agencies, we are enabled to develop and regulate the bodily functions of the idiot, to arouse his observation, to quicken his power of thought, and thus develop the sensitive and perceptive faculties; and we have not only succeeded in raising these poor creatures from a state of hopeless degradation to a state of comfort and usefulness, but we have, in many instances, succeeded in kindling up in their dark and twilight minds some dim anticipations of a brighter world; the veil which obscured their intellect has been rendered transparent, and to use the language of the bard of Avon, we have been privileged to observe that—
"As the morning steals upon the night,
Melting the darkness, so their rising senses
Begin to chase the ignorant fumes that mantle
Their clearer reason."
In addition to the Asylum proper, the Board has lately purchased a farm-house with 32 acres of land, immediately adjoining the main building. By means of this welcome acquisition, increased accommodation is afforded, and facilities are given for drafting off some of the most tractable patients who require less supervision than the majority of the inmates; moreover, farm work has proved very useful in training some of the patients who come from agricultural districts.
Crossley House.—Our area of usefulness has recently been extended by the munificent gift of Sir Savile Crossley, Bart., of a Convalescent Home, at Clacton-on-Sea. The building has accommodation for twenty patients; it stands facing the sea, in its own grounds of nearly an acre, and its privacy is secured by a walled-in garden, in which the inmates are able to take ample exercise. As a large number of our patients suffer from scrofula, or from some tubercular disease, the want has been long felt of a seaside adjunct, where such patients could be treated in the initial stage. Thanks to Sir Savile Crossley's princely gift, we now possess this valuable addition to our medical resources, the advantages of which cannot be too highly estimated.
The Ladies' Association.—The valuable additions that have recently been made to the Asylum, thus largely increasing the accommodation for patients, have necessarily entailed a largely increased expenditure, which could not have been met by the current income, had not the ladies of East Anglia come forward with great earnestness to help the objects of this Asylum by individual and energetic efforts; and one of the most interesting events of the last few years has been the formation of a Ladies' Association, the establishment of which is entirely due to the earnest and devoted efforts

of the Marchioness of Bristol. Its object is to disseminate information respecting the working of the Asylum, to secure admission for necessitous cases, and to organise and carry out annually house to house collections for its funds. H.R.H. the Princess of Wales has given her countenance to this movement by graciously accepting the office of Patroness, several influential ladies have consented to act as presidents over the various districts into which the four counties have been divided, and as many as 1,400 ladies are engaged in this philanthropic work.

CROSSLEY HOUSE, CLACTON-ON-SEA. CROSSLEY HOUSE, CLACTON-ON-SEA.

The success attending this movement has been phenomenal. During the first year of its operation, the substantial sum of £1,868 6s. 10d. was handed over to the general fund, this amount having been obtained from upwards of 20,000 contributors, who had thus the opportunity of joining in this good work, and whose aid could not have been secured in any other way. The efforts of these charitable ladies have been crowned with such signal success, that the large sum of £9,473 5s. 9d. has been added to the funds of the Asylum.[53] This substantial help is very gratifying to the Directors of the Institution, who now rely upon the Ladies' Association for nearly a fourth part of their income; and it is not too much to say that the future success of the Asylum is intimately connected with the continuance of the efforts of these philanthropic ladies, who seem to me to be influenced by the noble sentiments lately expressed by one of their number, that "The simple obligation of all thoughtful women, is that of making the world within our reach the better for our being, and gladder for our human speech. It is a work such as this that I am sure stirs us up to feel that we must also give our help, our sympathy, our lives for other people, and in this work lies the elements of unselfishness."[54]

All honour to these ladies, who, having learnt the elementary truth that privileges involve responsibilities, instead of hiding their talents in the napkin of selfishness, prefer to go forth as messengers of mercy, to try and flash the electric fire of philanthropy into the slumbering hearts of others, and to induce them to join in their grand and good work. They thus become a force and a factor of influence with all around them, and their reward will be the satisfaction of feeling that they are contributing their part in the great work of elevating these stricken members of our race, from their present unhappy and degraded condition to a higher position in the scale of created intelligence.

I trust I have said enough to show that the idiot ought and must be cared for; and in asking for your support, I will also ask you whether anything can be more gratifying than, as the result of scientific treatment, to see the idiot standing erect, asserting his birthright, and claiming brotherhood with the rest of the human family.

True philanthropy never stops short of the remotest boundary of human want, and in urging upon you the claims of the Eastern Counties' Asylum for Idiots, I would have you remember that I am pleading for a class who cannot plead for themselves, and whose very silence is eloquent with an appeal for your merciful aid.

Remember that these poor stricken individuals are members of the human family. They are heirs with us of all that human beings may hope for from the hands of a common Father. They possess the rudiments of all human attributes, especially the distinctive attribute of educability and of progressive improvement; their bodies are the vehicles which carry souls never destined to perish, through the series of ages, and when the walls of the cottages of clay in which their better part has sojourned collapse, and they mingle with their kindred dust, the freed inhabitants shall wing their way to brighter regions and to a more enduring home, and will thus illustrate the beautiful sentiment of one of our modern poets, when he said:

"In death's unrobing room we strip from round us

This garment of mortality and earth,

And breaking from the embryo-state which bound us,

Our day of dying is our day of birth."

Each person here belongs to one of two classes. Either you have one of these unhappy beings in your own immediate circle, or you have not. If you have, you can feel all the more for those who are similarly afflicted with yourselves, but have not your means for mitigating their dire distress, and you will think of the narrow home of the humble artisan or labourer, rendered intolerable by the constant presence of one of these afflicted members of our race. If, on the other hand, you have been spared this overwhelming calamity in your own family, and have had the joy of watching the dawn of infant intelligence, and have experienced the delight of seeing the capacities shown in the early life of your own children gradually ripen and develop into the intelligence of manhood, you will look with an eye of pity on the numerous households rendered miserable by the intolerable incubus of the presence in their midst of an idiot child, and will, I am sure, consider any assistance you can render to so good a cause in the light of a thank-offering.

The wear and tear of an excitable idiot child has wrecked many a family and reduced it to pauperism, for not only is such child a dead weight on the material prosperity of the family, but the hands of those who have to work for their livelihood, are sadly tied and hampered, when such an inmate has to be constantly looked after in the home; the labour by which the household is supported is often interrupted by one who can contribute nothing to the common stock, and the time which is so precious to hard-working people must, in part at all events, be occupied in caring for the one, who, if uncared for and neglected, must sink lower in the social scale and fall into a still more degraded condition. The care and treatment of the idiot, therefore, becomes a vital question of Political Economy; for by relieving a household of the burden and anxiety incident to the care of the afflicted child, the parents are enabled to devote all their energies to the support of their family. Moreover, there is often a moral aspect corresponding with the mental aspect of this question, and the presence of an idiot often becomes a source of real danger. Our able superintendent, Mr. Turner, in his interesting report for the year 1895, has illustrated the terrible anxiety caused by the presence of an idiot child in the homes of the poor, by the history of an inmate of our Asylum, who, when at home, being left to mind the baby, blacked its face all over with soot, so that when his mother returned, she might think she had a black baby. On another occasion, his little sister wanted some water, and he told her to drink out of the kettle on the fire, by which she nearly lost her life. This boy, who was evidently a type of the mischievous class of idiots, was once turned out of the Parish Church during service, for pricking another boy with a pin, so that he yelled out and disturbed the whole congregation. Two cases of murder by idiots have been recorded in a report of the Commissioners on Idiocy to the General Assembly of Connecticut; an idiot girl, being left alone with an infant, killed it by striking it on the head with a flat iron; and another vicious idiot killed a man who was working with him, by striking him on the head with a shovel. Esquirol also records the case of an idiot in the Salzburg Hospital, who killed a man by severing his head from his body with a hatchet, and then calmly seated himself by the side of the dead body.[55]

Philanthropists of the Eastern Counties of England, many of you have been long accustomed to sympathise with suffering and want; here is another outlet for your charitable efforts. The most illustrious landowner in East Anglia has recently extended his Royal patronage to this institution, especially established for the care of idiots from the four counties of Norfolk, Suffolk, Essex, and Cambridgeshire; and his Royal Consort the Princess of Wales has most graciously consented to accept the position of Patroness of the Ladies' Association, thus showing the deep interest that is felt by their Royal Highnesses in this important Eastern Counties' Charity. I ask you to follow their noble example; I ask you to come and help us in our attempts to rescue a large section of the human family from the worse than Cimmerian darkness in which they have been hitherto enshrouded; come and help us to awaken faculties hitherto dormant, to restore lost minds, to arouse these unhappy beings from a moral death to a new birth of perception and feeling; come and help us in arousing the slumbering power to utterance, and you shall hear the once silent tongue eloquent with the outgushings of a liberated spirit.

In conclusion, I wish to reiterate and to emphasise the statement, that these unfortunate members of the human family possess the tripartite nature of man—body, soul, and spirit—σωμα, ψυχη, πνευμα; they have the germ of intellectual activity and of moral responsibility, and this germ, cherished and nourished by the genial warmth of human kindness, fenced round and protected from the blasts and buffetings of the world by the cords of true philanthropy, watered by the dew of human sympathy, although possibly only permitted to bud here, is destined hereafter to expand into a perfect flower, and flourish perennially in another and a better state of being.

"Eternal process moving on,
From state to state the spirit walks.
All these are but the shattered stalks
Or ruined chrysalis of one."

FOOTNOTES

[1] See an interesting article on Idiocy, by Dr. Langdon Down, "Quain's Dictionary of Medicine." Vol. I., p. 926.

[2] "Idiocy and Imbecility," by W.W. Ireland, M.D. P. 36.

[3] I am glad to find that this question of the depletion of our workhouses is engaging the attention of Boards of Guardians, as shown by a meeting lately held in Norwich, to consider the propriety of reducing the number of workhouses in the district. At this conference, which was attended by delegates from various unions, Mr. Bartle H.T. Frere stated that the Aylsham workhouse, originally built for 619 persons, had never had more than 117 inmates during the past eleven years; and that in other unions, not more than a quarter of the actual workhouse accommodation was utilized, although a complete staff of officials was kept in each union. Mr. Frere pointed out the folly of keeping up such elaborate machinery, for such totally inadequate results, and that an enormous saving would be effected by the amalgamation of two or more unions for the purpose of housing their pauper population.

[4] This term is applied by the Greek writers to a person unpractised or unskilled in anything—one who has no professional knowledge, whether of politics or any other subject, and it seems to have corresponded with our word layman; thus, Thucydides, in describing the plague that broke out at Athens during the Peloponnesian War, in speaking of a physician and a layman, uses the phrase ιατρος καί ίσιωτης; Plato also uses the word in the same sense (Legg. 933 D), and the same author, in contrasting a poet with a prose-writer, uses the phrase, "εν μέτρω ώς ποιητης, ή άυευ μέτρου ώς ισιωτης" (Phaedr. 258 D). I doubt very much the appropriateness of the

word idiot as applied to these unfortunate creatures, and I think the American term of Feeble-minded more correctly represents their condition.

[5] The question of the influence of alcoholic stimulants on the development of mental disease formed a prominent feature in the proceedings of this congress, and it is also a subject which is just now engaging the attention of pathologists in all parts of the world.

[6] "Mentally-deficient Children, their treatment and training." By G.E. Shuttleworth, M.D. Page 36.

[7] Toussenel, a French writer, says "La plupart des idiots sont des enfants procréés dans l'ivresse bacchique. On sait que les enfants se ressentent généralement de l'influence passionelle qui a présidé à leur conception." At a discussion at the Obstetrical Society, Dr. Langdon Down is reported to have entertained similar views.

[8] I would refer those who may wish to pursue the inquiry as to the baneful influence of alcohol on the human frame, to the celebrated Cantor Lectures on Alcohol, by my friend Sir B.W. Richardson, in which he introduces the physiological argument into the temperance cause, asserting that alcohol cannot be classified as a food; that degeneration of tissues is produced, that it neither supplies matter for construction nor production of heat, but, on the contrary, militates against both. Sir B.W. Richardson's latest views upon this subject are developed in the pages of the "Hospital" for February 1st and March 14th, of this present year.

In France, M. Lunier, Inspector of Asylums, has shown that the departments in which the consumption of alcohol had increased most, were those in which there had been a corresponding increase of insanity, and this was shown most strikingly in regard to women, at the period when the natural wines of the country gave way to the consumption of spirits.

In Sweden, Dr. Westfelt has lately made a communication to the Stockholm Medical Society, containing the statistics of alcoholic abuse and its results in Sweden. He calculates that at least from 7 to 12 or 13 per cent. among males, and from 1 to 2 per cent. among females, of all cases of acquired insanity, are due to the abuse of alcohol; and in reference to its influence on progeny and race, he shows that a steady diminution of the population was coincident with a period when drunkenness was at its greatest height.

[9] "On the Causes of Idiocy." By S.G. Howe, M.D. Page 35.

[10] "Op cit," page 19.

[11] That eminent clinical observer, the late Professor Trousseau, in treating of the influence of consanguine marriages, gives the history of a Neapolitan family, in which an uncle married his niece. There had previously been no hereditary disease in the family; of the four children, the issue of this marriage, the eldest daughter was very eccentric; the second child, a boy, was epileptic; the third child very intelligent; and the fourth was an idiot and epileptic. "Clinique Médicale de l'Hôtel-Dieu de Paris." Tome ii., page 87.

[12] "New Facts and Remarks concerning Idiocy," by E. Séguin, M.D., p. 28. Dr. Séguin has been a voluminous contributor to the literature of Idiocy, and for many years his writings were the only available source of information on the management and education of idiots.

[13] Sir J.C. Browne, in speaking of the brain of men and women, says there can be no question of inferiority or superiority between them any more than there can be between a telescope and a microscope; but they are differentiated from each other in structure and function, and fitted to do different kinds of work in the world. He maintains that the weight of the brain is less in women than in men, that the specific gravity of the grey matter is less, that the distribution of the blood varies in the two sexes to a considerable extent, and that the blood going to the female brain is somewhat poorer in quality than that going to the male brain, and contains four millions and a half corpuscles to the cubic millimetre, instead of five millions in the case of the male.

[14] It seems that one of their own sex is of a different opinion, as in a series of articles in the "Nineteenth Century" for 1891 and 1892, Mrs. Lynn Linton strongly deprecates any departure from the comparatively restricted area of usefulness hitherto open to women, and she even baldly states that it is for maternity that women primarily exist! She also adds, "be it pleasant or unpleasant, it is none the less an absolute truth—the raison d'être of a woman is maternity ... the cradle lies across the door of the polling booth and bars the way to the senate."

In a powerful article in the same serial, entitled "Defence of the so-called Wild Women," Mrs. Mona Caird severely criticises Mrs. Lynn Linton's views as to the restrictions she would impose upon the freedom of women to choose their own career.

[15] Although the injurious effects of overpressure in education have been principally referred to in the education of girls, the same pernicious results may accrue in the case of boys. Dr. Wynn Westcott, in his work on "Suicide," states that during the last few years there have been several English cases of children killing themselves because unable to perform school tasks. He also says that child-suicide is increasing in England and in almost all Continental states, and that the cause in many cases is due to overpressure in education. Dr. Strahan, writing upon the same subject, in his treatise on "Suicide and Insanity," corroborates Dr. Westcott's views, and remarks that fifty years ago, child-suicide was comparatively rare; but that during the last quarter of a century it has steadily increased in all European states, and that the high-pressure system of education is generally considered as the cause of it.

If any apology be needed for dwelling at such length on the evils of the educational overpressure so prevalent in our days, I would observe that it has an indirect bearing upon the causation of idiocy; for although the sinister results recorded by Drs. Westcott and Strahan may be comparatively rare, still, consequences of a more remote character may ensue, for the injury done to the nervous system is cumulative and transmissible from generation to generation, and a neurotic tendency may be engendered in the offspring of those who have been exposed to this evil, which may manifest itself in the appearance of idiocy or some lesser form of mental defect.

[16] One of the most distinguished French psychologists, has thus expressed himself on this point:—"Dans des réunions ou l'idiotisme étendait son triste niveau, il m'est arrivé plusieurs fois de rencontrer des crânes, qui dans leur partie frontale eussent fait honneur aux hommes les plus justement célèbres, et où l'on eût pu trouver avec avantage les organes de toutes les sortes d'esprit, de celui même qui apprend à rire des mystifications et des sots."—Rejet de l'Organologie Phrénologique, par F. Lelut, p. 196.

[17] Dr. Wilmath, of the Pennsylvania Institution for Feeble-minded, reports that in six brains the island of Reil was exposed through defective development of the 3rd frontal convolution; in four cases, on both sides; in two cases, on one side only.—Notes on the Pathology of Idiocy.

[18] Il Cervello in Relazione con i Fenomeni Psichici. Studio sulla morfologia degli emisferi cerebrali dell'uomo, Torino, 1895. P. 89.

This is a work of great merit, in which the author compares the structure of the brain of man with that of other primates; he then treats of the morphology of the brain in different races, in criminals, in the insane, in deaf mutes, and in microcephales. An extremely interesting chapter is that devoted to the assumed difference of the cerebral hemispheres in the two sexes, containing statistical tables constructed by Dr. Mingazzini himself and others. Although he mentions certain minor differences that have been noticed by different observers, he summarises his own opinion by the statement that, "from the numerous but incomplete observations upon this subject, it may be concluded with certainty that essential differences do not exist" (si può inferire quasi con certezza che differenze essenziali non esistono).

[19] Further information as to brain weight and cranial capacity, will be found in the author's treatise on "Aphasia and the Localisation of Articulate Language," chapter xii. (Prize Essay of the Academy of Medicine of France.)

[20] Op. cit., page 64.

[21] The attention of the medical profession has lately been called to the obstetric aspect of idiocy, and I would refer those who take an interest in this subject to the valuable statistics of Dr. Langdon Down, which contain the result of his inquiries into the history of 2,000 cases of idiocy that have come under his observation; from which it would seem that primogeniture

plays an important part, as no less than 24 per cent. of all the idiot children observed were primiparous. The increased difficulty of parturition seemed to be an important factor. In reference to the use of the forceps in delivery as an assigned cause of idiocy, Dr. Down says, "there is no evidence that instrumental interference has any injurious influence on the mental condition of the children, but he thinks that those who delay the use of the forceps incur a much greater risk from the prolongation of pressure, resulting in suspended animation, which condition should be especially avoided. Of Dr. Down's 2,000 cases, the ratio of males to females was 2·1 to 0·9. This was probably due to the larger size of the head giving rise to the prolonged and difficult parturition, continued pressure, and suspended animation."—Obstetrical Journal, vol. iv., p. 681.

[22] Dr. Hammond, Professor of Diseases of the Nervous System at Bellevue College, New York, has published some interesting statistics in reference to the relative weight of the brain, as compared with that of the body, in various classes of vertebrate animals, by which he shows that there is no definite relation between the intelligence of animals and the absolute or relative size of the brain. Thus, he says, "the canary bird and the Arctic sparrow have brains proportionately larger than those of any other known animals, including man, and yet no one will contend that these animals stand at the top of the scale of mental development. Man, who certainly stands at the head of the class of mammals, and of all other animals, so far as mind is concerned, rarely has a brain more than one-fiftieth the weight of the body, a proportion which is much greater in several other mammals, and is, as we have seen, exceeded by many of the smaller birds."

[23] Clinical Lecture on Idiocy, p. 14.

[24] L'Encéphale, March 1881, p. 82.

[25] At a meeting of the Medico-Psychological Society of Paris, my friend M. Auguste Voisin exhibited plates of the brains of idiots who had only begun to speak at the age of from three to five years, in which the frontal and first parietal convolutions were rectilinear without secondary folds, resembling the fœtal condition of the convolutions at the sixth month of intra-uterine life.

[26] The imagination of certain psychologists seems to have gone rampant upon this subject; one writer, M. Moreau, of Tours, maintained that genius was a nervous disease—"le génie est une névrose"; and in order that there may be no mistake about his meaning, he adds that "the constitution of many men of genius is in reality the same as that of idiots!" M. Moreau's doctrine may thus be summarised in his own words:—"Les dispositions d'esprit qui font qu'un homme se distingue des autres hommes par l'originalité de ses pensées et de ses conceptions, par son excentricité on l'énergie de ses facultés affectives, par la transcendance de ses facultés intellectuelles, prennent leur source dans les mêmes conditions organiques

que les divers troubles moraux, dont la folie et l'idiotie sont l'expression la plus complète."

[27] Le Cerveau et la Pensée, par Paul Janet Membre de l'Institut. Paris, 1867, p. 58. This learned treatise contains an immense deal of information in reference to the mysterious connection between matter and mind, and I have found it of great service to me in my psychological researches.

[28] "Nineteenth Century," March, 1880, p. 509.

[29] "Darwinism Tested by Language," Rivington, 1877; "Aphasia or Loss of Speech, and the Localisation of the Faculty of Language," 2nd edition, Churchills, 1890. The reader is referred to these treatises, and especially to his work on Darwinism, for a fuller exposition of the author's views, here only incidentally sketched; and also for a more complete knowledge of the scientific facts and different authorities quoted in support of the position here taken in reference to the connection between Matter and Mind.

[30] "Das Leben ist nur ein besonderer, und zwar der complicirteste Act der Mechanik; ein Theil der Gesammtmaterie tritt von Zeit zu Zeit aus dem gewöhnlichen Gange ihrer Bewegungen heraus in besondre organisch-chemische Verbindungen, und nachdem er eine Zeit lang darin verharrt hat, kehrt er weider zu den allgemeinen Bewegungsverhältnissen zurück."— Gesammte Abhandlungen zu wissenschaftlicher Medicin s. 25.

[31] One of the leaders of scientific thought in this country tells us that "Life is composed of ordinary matter, differing from it only in the manner in which its atoms are aggregated," and it has been gravely stated that the production of man in the chemist's retort may be recorded as one of the future discoveries of the age!

A clever French writer, commenting on these purely hypothetical statements of the "mechanistic school," makes the following appropriate remarks:—

"Quand on nous dit que l'organisme des êtres vivants n'est qu'un laboratoire où tout se passe en combinaisons et en compositions des éléments matériels primitifs, on oublie que ce laboratoire est habité par un hôte intime, le principe vital qui ne fait qu'un avec les éléments en fusion. Ici la combinaison chimique ne se fait pas toute seule; elle s'opère sous l'action d'une cause qui en transforme les éléments de façon à en faire un produit d ordre nouveau qui s'appelle la vie."—"La Vie et la Matière," par E. Vacherot, Revue des Deux Mondes," 1878.

[32] In an original and very remarkable essay, entitled "The Brain not the Sole Organ of the Mind," Dr. Hammond, of New York, says, "There is no exception to the law that mental development is in direct proportion to the amount of grey matter entering into the composition of the nervous system of any animal of any kind whatever; and that in estimating mental power, we should be influenced by the absolute and relative quantity of grey nerve tissue, in which respect we shall find man stands pre-eminent, although, as

we have already seen, his brain, as a whole, is relatively much smaller than that of many other animals; and it is to this preponderance of grey matter that Man owes the great mental development which places him so far above all other living beings. As this grey tissue is not confined to the brain, but a large proportion of it is found in the ganglia of the sympathetic and some other nerves, and as an amount second only to that of the brain in quantity—and, indeed, in some animals larger—is present as an integral constituent of the spinal cord, Dr. Hammond infers, and he cites numerous experiments in support of this inference, that mental power must be conceded to the spinal cord, and that the brain can no longer be considered as the sole organ of the mind."

[33] "The Physical Basis of Mind." Page 441.

[34] The late Bishop of Carlisle illustrates the independence of the Ego, by an allusion to moral feelings. "A murderer," he says, "is convicted twenty years after the offence had been committed, or he gives himself up after so many years, because his memory and his conscience make his life miserable. He has no doubt as to the fact that the person who did the deed of darkness years ago, is the same person as he who feels the pangs of remorse to-day. Every material particle in his body may have changed since then, but there is a continuity in his spiritual being out of which he cannot be argued, even if any ingenious sophist should attempt the task."—Nineteenth Century, March, 1880, p. 510.

[35] To those who may wish to pursue this subject further, I recommend a perusal of an essay on "Materialistic Physiology," in the Journal of Psychological Medicine for April, 1877. In this article, the writer, Dr. Winn, seems to share my views as to the paramount importance of boldly facing this matter, when he says:—

"The unphilosophical and extravagant dogma, that matter can think, is now so loudly and confidently asserted, and so widely spread by a numerous class of medical men and physiologists, both in this country and abroad, that the time has arrived when a doctrine so fallacious, and so fraught with danger to the best interests of society, should be fairly and carefully scrutinised. It is not by mere assertion, or the use of obscure and pedantic language, that such a theory can be established; and if it can be shown that the arguments on which it is based are shallow and speculative, words can scarcely be found too strong to censure the recklessness and folly of those who promulgate views so subversive of all morality and religion.

"The physicists have utterly failed to establish their position. They were asked to prove by inductive reasoning the truth of their theory, that the universe is the mere outcome of molecular force, and their defence has been clearly proved to be of the most evasive and inconclusive character.

"The doctrines of the modern school of materialistic physiology are permeating all classes of society, and it is these doctrines, based on the assumption that mind is a mere function of the brain—an assumption that, if true, would reduce man to the level of the beasts that perish—that we are offered as a substitute for the belief in the immateriality of the mind."

The essay from which the above quotations are taken is full of sound and logical reasoning, and the writer's position is not supported by mere theoretical statements, but by arguments drawn from well-accredited facts in anatomy and physiology.

[36] I strongly deprecate, as lamentably wrong and needless, the violent language sometimes used by writers on both sides of this great controversy of the origin of man. If the odium theologicum may have inspired some of the opponents of evolution, it is undeniable that there is strong evidence of an odium antitheologicum amongst not a few of the supporters of this doctrine, who indulge in abusive epithets, launching into personalities of a most objectionable kind; for instance, we are informed that "orthodoxy is the Bourbon of the world of thought; it learns not, neither can it forget." Now I protest against the attempt to obscure argument by appeals to the passions and to prejudice. Science and Theology should not be regarded as two opposing citadels, frowning defiance upon each other, but their votaries should look upon each other as co-labourers in the cause of truth, and they should welcome light and knowledge from whatever quarter it may come, being fully convinced that all systems and theories irreconcilable with truth, are built upon the sand, and must ultimately be swept away.

[37] One of our popular novelists, Sir Walter Besant, has philosophically said, "there is between the condition of Man and the Brute an interdependence which cannot but be recognised by every physician. So greatly has this connection affected some of the modern physicians, as to cause doubt in their minds whether there be any life at all hereafter; or if when the pulse ceases to beat, the whole man should become a dead and senseless lump of clay. In this they confuse the immortal soul with the perishable instruments of brain and body, through which in life it manifests its being and betrays its true nature, whether of good or evil."—Faith and Freedom.

[38] Cases like this would seem to illustrate the truth of the statement of that great philosopher, Sir Thomas Browne, when he says, "Thus it is observed that men sometimes, upon the hour of their departure, do speak and reason about themselves. For then the soul, being more freed from the ligaments of the body, begins to reason like herself, and to discourse in a strain above mortality."—Religio Medici, p. 208.

[39] A society has lately been formed under the name of "The National Association for promoting the welfare of the Feeble-minded," the object of which is to establish homes for defective and feeble-minded children of a class more highly-endowed with intelligence than those who would be received into an ordinary idiot asylum; statistics having shown that

ignorance and mental dulness tend to crime in various forms. Without expressing any very decided opinion upon the above project, it seems to me that the unnecessary multiplication of charitable institutions is itself an evil, and is not calculated to promote efficiency or economy; and if special provision is made for those just above the highest class of idiots, as is proposed, the present Idiot Asylums must necessarily suffer. Without, therefore, in any way disparaging the above scheme, I would suggest great caution in reference to it, as it is impolitic and unwise to make fresh demands upon a philanthropic public, unless the need for it is clearly established, as the result must inevitably be the diversion of funds from existing institutions already doing a good and charitable work.

[40] Maladies Mentales, Tome ii., p. 76, par E. Esquirol, médecin en chef de la maison royale des aliénés de Charenton. "Les idiots sont ce qu'ils doivent être pendant tout le cours de leur vie. On ne conçoit pas la possibilité de changer cet état. Rien ne saurait donner aux malheureux idiots, même pour quelques instants, plus de raison, plus d'intelligence."

[41] "Mentally deficient children," page 110.

[42] This painstaking observer has investigated this subject in an interesting communication on Sporadic Cretinism in the "Edinburgh Medical Journal" for May, 1893. Dr. Ireland considers Sporadic Cretinism to be a congenital or infantile form of myxœdema, and bearing in mind the increasing mental torpor which has followed the ablation of the thyroid gland performed by Kocher, and the cretinoid condition induced in monkeys by the removal of the thyroid by Horsley, he is drawn to the conclusion that this gland secretes and pours something into the blood which has a powerful effect upon the nutrition and function of the brain, and of the whole organism, and these views receive a certain amount of confirmation from the fact that in most cases of Sporadic Cretinism the thyroid gland is totally wanting. Dr. Ireland also expresses the opinion, in which I fully concur, that there is too much solidism in our pathology, and that the vital powers of the blood have been too much overlooked.

Although the effect of thyroid treatment in the idiot is still sub judice, there is overwhelming testimony of its value in Myxœdema, an allied affection; and I would refer those who desire further information upon this matter to an important discussion at the Edinburgh Medico-Chirurgical Society, in February, 1893, arising out of papers read by Professor Greenfield, Dr. Byrom Bramwell, Dr. Lundie, Dr. Dunlop, and Dr. John Thomson, when important additions were made to the literature of this affection by Dr. Affleck, Dr. George Murray, and others, whose matured views will form a valuable contribution to our knowledge of this somewhat obscure subject.

[43] "Pediatrics," May, 1896, p. 460.

[44] I give M. Voisin's description of the symptoms in his own words. "Elle est arrivée dans mon service en état d'extase mystique, exécutant

continuellement des mouvements de ses deux mains, surtout de la droite, semblables à ceux d'une personne en prière; elle porte souvent les mains à son front comme pour faire le signe de la croix. Elle murmure des mots, entre autres, Ave Maria. La physiognomie exprime la douleur mêlée d'extase."

[45] "Edinburgh Medical Journal," May, 1893, p. 1053.

[46] "Edinburgh Hospital Reports," Vol. 3, 1895, p. 245. "This is the most complete monograph on thyroid treatment that has come under my notice. Dr. Bramwell has recorded, in minute detail, the clinical history of twenty-three cases of myxœdema, and five cases of sporadic cretinism."

[47] "Journal of Mental Science," April, 1895, p. 280.

[48] "British Medical Journal," Jan. 30th, and Feb. 6th, 1892, "Remarks on the Function of the Thyroid Gland." I recommend a careful perusal of this important and exhaustive essay of Professor Horsley to all those who desire to acquaint themselves with what is known about the structure and functions of the thyroid gland; for it will be remembered that it is to the experiments on animals by this learned and accomplished scientist, that we are principally indebted for our knowledge of the connection between myxœdema and loss of function of the thyroid gland.

[49] "Traitement et Education des Enfants Idiots et Dégénérés," p. 241, par M. Bourneville, Médecin de Bicêtre, Paris, 1895. The author of the above treatise is one of the most prolific French writers on Idiocy, and I desire to call especial attention to that part of the work which embraces the Medico-Pedagogic Treatment of Idiocy. In this section, M. Bourneville describes in minute detail the gymnastic and physical training adopted at Bicêtre, the description being copiously illustrated by plates, which cannot fail to interest those engaged in the treatment of idiocy.

[50] "Journal of Anatomy and Physiology," January, 1895, p. 304.

[51] "Pediatrics," March, 1896, p. 243.

[52] "On Idiocy and Imbecility," page 91.

[53] As showing the result of individual effort, I may mention that in the year 1894, as much as £155 0s. 7d. was collected in the N. Walsham District, £89 12s. 9d. in the Norwich District, and £80 15s. 6d. in the Diss District, under the presidentship respectively of Mrs. Petre, Lady Lade, and Mrs. Sancroft Holmes.

[54] The Countess of Warwick, at the "Young Helpers' League."

[55] Des Maladies Mentales, Tome ii., p. 103.